CAROLINA GHOST WOODS

CAROLINA GHOST WOODS

poems

JUDY JORDAN

LOUISIANA STATE UNIVERSITY PRESS ✵ Baton Rouge

MM

Manufactured in the United States of America
First printing
09 08 07 06 05 04 03 02 01 00
5 4 3 2 1

Designer: Amanda McDonald Scallan
Typeface: Sabon
Printer and binder: Thomson-Shore, Inc.

Library of Congress Cataloging-in-Publication Data
Jordan, Judy, 1961–
    Carolina ghost woods : poems / Judy Jordan.
    p. cm.
    ISBN 0-8071-2555-5 (cloth : alk. paper) — ISBN 0-8071-2556-3 (paper : alk. paper)
    I. Title.

PS3560.0729 C37 2000
811' .54—dc21

99-057981

The author gratefully acknowledges the editors of the following publications, in which some of the poems herein first appeared, some in slightly different form: *Crossroads:* "Silences"*; Poet Lore:* "At Winter's Edge," "Saying My Prayers," "A Taste for Falling"; *Poetry:* "In the 25th Year of My Mother's Death"; *Third Coast:* "Scattered Prayers"; *Western Humanities Review:* "Carolina Ghost Woods," "Two Hours before Sunrise," "Walking the Geese Home," "Winter"; *Writer's Eye:* "Help Me to Salt, Help Me to Sorrow."
    "In the 25th Year of My Mother's Death" and "A Taste for Falling" were published in limited edition, hand-printed broadsides at the McGuffey Arts of the Book Center, Charlottesville, Virginia.

The author is especially grateful to the Virginia Commission for the Arts, the Henry Hoynes Foundation, and the Steffensen Cannon Foundation for Fellowships, without which these poems could never have been written. Thanks also to the faculty and students of the University of Virginia Creative Writing Program and the University of Utah Creative Writing Program for their support and suggestions.

Contents

THE SILENCE, THE BONE-WEARY SOUND

DREAM OF THE END

CAROLINA ALLOWANCE

Sharecropper's Grave
(for my grandmother)

The night is hoot owls, wind-whistled flue, babies bundled in burlap.
Breath of another child, mid-gasp.

In the next room, those who live
and the ones sickness took—the pail of milk,
thick and frothing, they did not drink.

Small holes, secret graves,
children scattered around the iron fence.
Not even a scratched stone.

The wind rises, clouds cover the moon,
a dog's bark and those owls,
alone and no end.

My children who won't hear.
The night full of cries they will never make.

Scattered Prayers
(CNHJ, 1927–1969)

Deep in the horned cave of the lacertilian winter,
in horse manure and sawdust, in straw and spilled oats,

                                        my mother waits.
One shovelful at a time
                she shatters the belly of the wheelbarrow.

I dig next season's garden, spread her inch deep
and in the morning find her whole again.
Sifting slug eggs and the seeds of henbit,
she's recumbent and redolent in the twisted roots.

In this world of memory, this world of prayers
                              tossed to the crows,
in the floods that bring the pale tongue of spring,
the field turned pond,
                she's the darkening waterline,
the foam's filth in scrub and spindle,
a signal in the black oak's highest fork.
                        My questions
shudder through leaf-scurf.

It's time's mirage,
              this world,
sleight-of-hand and the clown's dance,
the same questions and somewhere
                    answer enough.

                    ⌒

She knows we've lost the farm she worked her life for.
She hears the auctioneer's thin call,
                      the banker's paper shuffle.
In the shrink of light,
dirt falling from her hand,

the sun leaving the trees one by one,
she remembers seed rotted in the wet ground one year,
the next so dry even the weeds wouldn't grow.

She's the lone kitchen match
                              our house burnt for the insurance;
she's what's left—four chimneys
                              and sun breaking across the tin roof.

Match fret and the embers' breath;
whether I sleep or wake,
a firefly in the dark house
or the red light-swell behind my eyes,
                              it's her,
sticky as resin oozing from pine shelves,
drifting through the spears of aloes,
curled into Union Memorial's tarnished pudding bowl.
The ballerina in the black-lacquered box,
                              tinny plinks and a twirl,
tinny plinks and a twirl.

                    ⁀⟩

She swallowed a just-laid egg for conception,
bared her stomach to the full moon to ensure a girl this time.
A plowshare under her bed to cut the pain,
she drank a bottle of castor oil to ease me from between her legs.

Sifted flour, poured buttermilk,
tossed salt over her shoulder—
an offering to the devil,
an appeasement to the death-click of scuttle bugs.

She knew the hunger of ditchweed and possum fat,
took food to the black marchers the factory let go,
got herself fired when she drove her friend Jo-Anne to town,
paid the doctor and bought the newborn's medicine.

3

She knew which forked branch for dowsing,
how many feet down for water,
which stump, the time of moon, the words for washing away warts.

I grow fat in the same places,
fit my hands to the smoothed handle of her hoe,
dry apples on the tin roof,
and wrinkle in the same sun that saw her buried my seventh year.

Each summer I sell tomatoes at the farmer's market
further works her face from mine.
Faster now that I'm only ten years younger than she can ever be,
faster now that I live so many women in one body,
I, who have never made a life within myself.

Between last and first frost
the weighted branches disjoin.
With a scrape and a bow,
apples pitch to the earth's swell
and squint from the blue-eyed grass.

She won't be tempted.
Not the buttermilk biscuits and sweet tea,
not the empty dress grown to the hanger's shape,
but takes a sock, my shoe laces,
the sleeve of a favorite shirt.
                              Lost in a flooded creek,
there's a kind of truth in a watery cuff;
somewhere in the rot-riddled fabric,
the trace of an answer that keeps me here
and keeps her, tickseed and leaves,
lifted and scattered,
                    strewn thus and not otherwise.

This is the time of year when she takes me from school
to glean the lowest branches of the cotton plant,
the time when each small wind shakes spiders to my open door.
Stunned by cold, salamanders,
raw as the crusted moon,
crouch on the unraked threshold. Splayed fingers and toes,

                                             then she's gone

into the blear light.

What can I know of the earth's turning,
                            its sustained desire,
or the way land falls away in flood,
then rises piece and bit through the churning debris,
through the writhing water's yellow gut,
through my baby teeth between the mattresses,
hair-tuft under her pillow,
her whispers to the thrown chicken bones.

Rises through the skiff's surge and strain
to hold my face between her floury hands.

In the Shadows

We stumbled down mourners' paths
between willows in full leaf,
tombstone to tombstone

toward a city, where a wife, the word
like persimmon skin in his mouth,
rattled pots, slammed closets.

His eyes were pale blue souls
lost between the body
and the three-day trail to God.

What do I care? It was just his hands
scraping against buttons and zippers,
the ground damp, pigeons angel to angel.

But I was learning, there in the absence of sun,
the worst of an hour struggled
in the shadow of stone wings.

Saying My Prayers

Hard to believe in any wrong this January.
Already we see the forsythia's first blooms,
their chances clear as the flash of ice scraps,
black with exhaust, skitting across pavement.

The passion of abandon is what the forsythia knows.
It defies this ice-covered city and ice molds my life,

something to be kicked through like the storm's debris,
something to curl into this night, waiting

on whatever comfort you might send.

Help Me to Salt, Help Me to Sorrow

In the moon-fade and the sun's puppy breath,
   in the crow's plummeting cry,
in my broken foot and arthritic joints,
                              memory calls me
to the earth's opening, the graves dug again, and again
I, always I am left
                    to turn away
into a bat's wing-brush of air.

That never changes . . .
   not this morning, not here

where I've just found
in the back of my truck, under the rubber mat,
in a teacup's worth of dirt,
where it seems no seed could possibly be,
a corn kernel split to pale leaves and string-roots.

It's a strange leap but I make it
and bend to these small harvests

because somewhere in North Carolina there was a house
   and in it my room and my bed,
bare boards and the bloodstains
that in each slant rain's worried whispers puddle to the cries of a slave,
murdered in 1863 when he tried to escape.

Somewhere there was a child who slept
on the living room's red-vinyl couch.

But I can't remember when the creek
   that bounded our family farm led to an ocean
or when a boxcar's weather-wasted letters spelling Illinois
   meant somewhere there was an Illinois.

It's still 1976—
the day after I've been seen playing tennis
  with a black boy, and it seems I will always
be held at gunpoint and beaten
as if the right punch would chunk out his name.

⌒)

No, it's 1969—
The year my mother becomes a wax paste
and I learn the funereal smell of carnations.
That year the moon was still made of green cheese.
That year men first bagged and labeled that moon.

⌒)

I still don't know why Odell Horne
  pulled a shotgun on my brother
  or how the body contains so much blood.
I still don't know why Donna Hill went to Myrtle Beach
and three days later came back dead.

For ten years I put up with Louise Stegall,
my father's girlfriend, one of her four men, all buried—
  suicide, murder, drink, again murder.
It was after the second one that she sat stock-still
and silent, four years in the asylum.
Now she walks the road all day,
picking up Cracker Jack trinkets
  to give to children
                brave enough to approach her.

When I was nine, the starling pecked outside her window a whole week.
Somebody's gonna die, she said
and made me hug Uncle Robert's neck
as if I couldn't know he'd be gone in two hours,
as if I hadn't learned anything about people
                and their vanishing.

9

The last time I saw her she wouldn't look at me,
  but jerked her sweatshirt's hood across her face
and stepped into the ditch,
as though there are some things even she won't tell,
as though I've never known it's dirt and dust after all—
the earth's sink and the worms' castings.

⁀

With the wet leaves thick on my steps,
the evening sky bruised dull gray to black,

when I've spilt salt and as the saying goes the sorrow and tears,
and the stove is cold so salt won't burn,
tell me my pocket of charms can counter any spell.

Tell me again the reason for my grandfather's fingers
afloat in the Mason jar on the fireplace mantel,
between the snuff tin and the bowl of circus peanuts.
What about the teeth in the dresser bureau,
the sliver of backbone I wear around my neck?

Again the washed-out photo in the family album,
Pacific wind lifting the small waves onto Coral Beach,
clicking the palm trees' fronds.
Again my father's rakish grin,
  his bayonet catching a scratch of sun,
his left foot propped on the stripped and bloodied body.

                                        Behind him, a stack of Japanese.

⁀

Let me believe in anything.
Doesn't the grizzled chicken dig up hoodoo hands?
Won't the blue door frame, the basket of acorns, protect me;
what about the knife in a pail of water?

When giving me the dead's slippered feet

                         room to room,

why not also synchronicity's proof,
  a wish and the tilted ears of angels?

I want to believe in the power of rosemary
knuckled along the fence
even as the stars order themselves
  to an unalterable and essential law.
I want the wind-whipped leaves to settle
  and the flattened scrub to right itself,
want the loose tin in the neighbor's shed

                              to finish its message.

When this season in its scoured exactitude shifts closer,
give me devil's blue boletus through the piled leaves,
the slender green of earthtongue,
phosphorescent honey tuft dispatched by the dead.

Their voices coming nearer, almost deciphered.

Whatever lies you have
there in that nail-clipping of time,

                        give them to me.

Prayers to My Mother

Day wound to a heel-spur in the yellow light of winter,
I cross this field of bones.

Never step on a grave, I know,
but I'm here as if there were some answer
in this field of scratched rocks and tombstones

where tangled souls
cast circles in the moonless cold
and each step sinks into ice.

It's not to the earth I turn but the sky,
that heavy coat tossed over the Carolinas' shoulders
as again tonight I send up words.

Come as if you hadn't lain pale in the pink lace,
as if I'd never witnessed the pulleys' groans,
never heard the scrape of shovel, the thud of clay.

As if I've never known how soon I'll become the land,
or how the dead move closer,
their blurred faces rising, hands reaching from their caves.

Come just this once, close so that I smell perfume,
see the snow's reflection off your teeth.

Long Drop to Black Water

What confidence led us into a rainy Ithaca night
neither I nor my friend knew. Swollen gorges
to our left, the ground crumbling
as we clung to tree trunks and hooked our fingers
into the tight loops of a gun factory fence,
sleighting a path in spray and fog
that swallowed our legs below the knees,
not knowing till the next day's retracking
how often we had hung, far from the eroded bank,
above nothing but a long drop to black water.

Whatever that confidence was, I've lost it.
But it informs the toads,
crouches them in crooked caves of alder roots,
pulses the pale skin under their slack mouths,
keeps them in the pond's tight waves clutching anything:
a pine's resinous knot, a fist of chair foam,
even a drowned and legless female.

Now in the sun's last light, unctuous through haze
that lifts the land above itself
and leans the alders over water in green flames,
I see more in the pasture's stubbed grass,
leaping sure and unwavering to the cold,
without thought of the ducks scouring the pond's edge
for the mass of eggs
or the snapper hungry on the gelid bottom.
What could bring them year after year
and always less in number
but faith in their own wholeness and desire.
Faith that I lack, faith that I want
in this spring, fecund and feral.

Carolina Ghost Woods

(for Charles Wright)

A crow calls and the sunset smears into questions
that swing with the cow's hoof, reflect in fire,
and wait under the wing with the thin lips of death.

Apple peel curls, silver yawn of doors,
the driven day's reek,
all swell and shrink in equal breaths
                              and tomorrow never comes.
Not to that world where the peacock fans its eyes
and the twelfth key unlocks the gate,
that place where I slid, my kidneys failed, heart slurred to a stop.
Yet I didn't die but blundered back
to the common and nameable, to doctors
telling my mother, *sorry, sorry, we couldn't* . . .

I don't know what power allowed my slip against the river's current
or how I could lie at the field's edge all that year
listening for the shift of roots.
I was so still squirrels and rabbits licked my skin
and I brought them home to my mother's sigh of *changeling*.
Some answer other than ghosts—

some answer other than we were all caught
in those woods of otherworldly drift,
that Carolina allowance
                      of the ease with which we shake from ourselves
and are lost on the path's dip,
lost where the water's slow rise becomes air,
                                    where I become air
and tremble above myself.

This world seeps across my life
more than anything I've ever touched.
It crouches me here in my knowledge,

14

palpable as the deer skull in the flower bed,
inscrutable as two birds fighting outside my house,
a crash through trees
                         and the muffled cry of the crow,
blood-spattered and staring at me with its single eye.

Tonight the clock is meaningless
and I'm still a child on the back steps,
my father gone into the woods to kill himself
while I wait for the single shotgun blast,
an echo of the wood's echo
that drags us out or tosses us back,

my father returning, days later,
not talking, dirt-scuffed and smelling of smoke.

In this land of ghosts and amulets,
where the bloodstain on the attic floorboards won't wash up
and locked doors fling themselves open,
here where my grandfather horsewhips the ten-foot-tall,
gap-mouthed thing up from the woods grabbing his mules' traces,
land where birds beat at my windows,
                                    where eaves are shifted
and the tin loosed with their wings,
                              land where people can kill themselves,
and return,
I need the tremor of my father's hands,
need to know how he won his way back,
need the single note of the blackbird in the hemlock
                                          not to twist
into another life ending.

Gnats are plucked from the bird's wing,
tomorrow blinked away in the crow's chalked eye

and tonight marked by blue graveyard lights,

and still I reach for that which everywhere
twitches into its other self.

Still I understand the words jostling
just out of hearing better than anything ever said.

Those who wait outside the frame
raise me each morning,
constant in their mist of absence.

They wait beside the cannas no one digs now,
in front of the footprints
no one left coming from the barnyard.

Foxfire daubs this night's swollen joints
with the seven-year-old's guilt,
the one who caught wild animals,
who didn't understand how death keeps count,
that birds are ferriers of the soul
or what a bird loosed indoors would mean,
who not one month before her mother would die
scooped the meadowlark from the river's bank
and released it in the house.

Nobody knows how close the land
where the black birds hunch on the tree's bare limbs,
but why not a sign?

When the leaves shudder to the muddy ground
and snow under the gutters puddles red,
when the bird lifts, the rabbit shivers in clumped grass
and the fox shrinks into the bramble,

when the shadow crosses the pitchfork's broken handle
and the hinges of the shed door rust,

                                   let me believe someone is there.

Because darkness flutters through chinks of thin walls
and I, not a semblance of movement in the dark woods,
drop, wet-eyed, not knowing if anyone will hear,
not knowing if a head should be bent ever so slightly
what such a listening would mean.

Because somewhere a bird clutches the scrap of my name.

ALONG AN UNSEEN EDGE

Killing at the Neighbors'

Never mind what you might think.
I was not so impressed by the way,
three bullets in him,
he hauled himself the stretch of sidewalk,
dizzying but catching on the car's hood,
leaving a perfect handprint,
then each step's larger mark of blood to the locked house
where he shouted to the child crouched behind the bed,
the two others in the closet,
his wife shoveling words to the black mouthpiece,
I shot my man. Send somebody—
till his own mouth soured around the words
and he dropped to the garage floor,
so even the chickens, who returned to their scratching
just out of reach of the dog,
who all day dragged his chain through shit
and the mud of the upset water bowl,

heard nothing. Never mind all that.
For what I slept with was the press of that brush,
just an old handleless used for whitewalls;
the ache of it in my palm
and my mother's insisting, *We don't want her
to come back to this. Scrub harder.*
What I slept with was not the taste of my chewed lip
but the memory of the green hose taut against the brick,
not the cold water, jeans-sucked up my thighs,
easing into my cupped hands,
but how the stains wouldn't come up,
just pinked, like candy fireballs licked to their core.

Now I lie down years later. She's back,
her children chasing me across the cement

21

in that old game of freeze
until I am tagged in the spot
where I had rubbed my five-year-old hands raw
and I wait, shallow-breathed, to be freed.

Through These Halls

Of course it's all over the morning news
so the school bus buzzes with it
and my classmates look at me

with that wide silence, interminable as the inch of mildew
board by board through the guinea shed,
then their eyes drop, as if crumbling with a groan to rust and rot.

Worse than the few who openly stare
after the sixth-grade teacher sends me
with a note to the principal's office.

Walking that hall, noticing the paper shows
no shadows of ink-slants and lines, I unfold
my own dread in the blank sheet,

knowing somewhere the news announcer
again drones on about the father shooting his son,
as my cousin is sponged by the undertaker's assistant

and my uncle shuffles to a damp cell,
maybe already thinking of the ripped shirt,
the slug-sweat of the bar he'll tie it to.

It doesn't matter whether I pocket that paper
and turn back to the now quiet class
or continue toward the office—

there's always the teacher hushing the students
and my slip through the wink of each window
carrying my pretext down that long, sun-slashed hall.

Hitchhiking into West Virginia

Even here in this dabbed and scumbled distance
the dead stow my name in the slack of their mouths.
I can wait forever in the pitch of this deserted road,
circling and staring, the twenty years
since my mother tried to shoot my brother

not mattering, the pistol's trigger pulled again
and again, the bullets striking ground
between my brother's feet. Even if
she never aimed at anything but dirt,
the twist of years has nothing to say
to the night layered on night
or his shirt stained and face blood-streaked
from where she rammed his head
twice into the trunk of an oak.

Hitchhiking for no reason
other than to be somewhere else,
I don't know if I should backtrack
along an unseen edge or continue,
pavement dipping and ascending, my brother
grabbing the empty pistol
and swinging his right fist to her face,
or should I hike further, to her death, one year later.

Either way, it's a narrow stretch of road.
The ground, without light to give it form,
rises against my feet
and rocks and trees brush past before words can mean anything.

Outside themselves,
the dead too,
nameless and without bound,
come closer, staking a claim.

A Taste for Falling

Maybe it was the cold pulling through darkness stippled on darkness,
washing the world loose so I walked untethered,
floating above the frost-traced stubble of corn
in the trembling night to the rock-ledge above water.

If there was a moon, it fell from my hands
into the wild flowers we call white tears,
fell through nights textured like dreams.

But there was no moon.
Only me hungry enough to peel bark from birch trees,

aware always of the river's slosh and drift,
aware always how the slightest movement
swallows you in cold's toothy grin.

Say I scaled the thin wind and joined the wild children of the woods,
learned the language of the orphaned dead,
got lost on the trail between worlds.

Say I forgot myself,
became a stutter of blue light
swirling in a river bottom's spiral,
my voice wet winter branches against a soot sky.

Say it's the fog of my breath that's wiped from windows,
my shadow sputtering at the screen.

$\backsim$

It was not the objects but what linked me to them.
Not the passage from side yard to post and wire,
past the cemetery, past the restless cows,
not the clumped thorn trees or catalpas chattering in wind,

but my mother's room, her perfume lingering,
years after her death.

Like a house I was a squabble of ghosts.
Things never mentioned slipped all night, bed to bed,
or, hobnailed, trod from hallway to kitchen
to stop three black linoleum squares from the sink.
Again the painting fell from the wall.
Again someone touched the needle to the record.

It buttoned me into night's skin,
this life of strange customs.
It seeped into my joints, wore my cartilage to flint,
woke me in a house of breathing,
an empty house full of breathing.

Eyes lit like jack-o'-lanterns slid across the field and I disappeared.

Twisted into the sky's whirl,
I didn't sate my hunger on sweet gum and stripped pine,
never ate pitch and needles,

didn't survive but one slack-mouthed night
the broken wing inside me opened to the river,
since when I've known nothing except a dream gone black,
a taste for falling, from which I never wake.

October

Because somewhere beyond the flood-cut bank
there's possibility and an answer.
Because somewhere, flung open,
one limb past the two squirrels
in the sycamore's top branches
I could step through the mockingbird's lone note,

I'm willing to crawl out on this water-slicked log
just to watch the sun climb the distant hill.
Yet another attempt to find what the guidebooks can't say
in this place smelling green-walnut bitter
and drifting up at each kicked leaf:
something that promises we will go on.

Maybe I'll remember the name of the pulpy-stemmed
purple orchids, unfolded under hardwoods,
their single leaves like curled palms with nothing to hold.
And I'll know how the locust so easily emerges
from the husk of its body, the snake its skin,
even the common damselfly from the nymph.

Then the world a fairy-tale,
those three gray stones on the sand-bank
the sons of Bairbre who rises from the water,
Prince Ferdia crashing through underbrush
on his black horse like nothing—

nothing that's ever enough.

A Short Drop to Nothing

I can't say what of this day or its lack
has caused me to weary on this floating dock
in the drift of the water's warp and wrest,
with the indifferent sun, that seed-heavy sack,
tremulous over the pines, spilling its chaff.

Geese lift from the far hill in the last light,
unfurl above alders, dip and scrape across the pond,
and I don't know how much longer I can wait
as the wind, smelling of leaf rot and dung,
tugs the evening over this darkening land.

Two Hours before Sunrise

Only he and I in the all-night deli
so I'm afraid to leave,
                    must listen
as he tells me about his spaceship stolen by NASA,
Nobel Prizes lost to politics,
medicine he doesn't need, sleep he hasn't had,
listen as he repeats, *all I need is a home-baked apple pie*
and a woman to rock me in her arms.

It's as if he knows I've seen those who mumble into their greasy coat sleeves,
the ones who grab pickles off the plates of the restaurant's uncleared tables,
shake out handfuls of salt, mumbling, "I've got to eat something"
then run into the street,

as if he knows I've risen in fog,
                            my third day without food,
knows I know what it is to be without a home
and to uncurl from sleep on a riverbank
like the trees uncurl from ice
and turn into a day that never held out its hands to me.

Though he says nothing about the maps of childhood,
                                    I've heard his story before.
The moths stain the streetlights with it,
rats whisper it to the foundation's knotty beams.

It's an ordinary story, though in the night unrecognizable,
                                        like the years
that have paused to rub their furred mouths against my leg and pass on.

                    ⌒⌐

Strange, the brain's leaps. The deli, then my cousin
who taught me to drive a column stick shift

in the rust-blotched Ford behind our grandmother's cabin, gets life.

Over the years things happened I don't understand,
                                    and he kills a roomful of men.

A twist in the chain of neurons
                    and he decapitates them.

Who's to say what curves and u-turns haunted him,
which smudges on that strange map he couldn't follow
so the same night he'd leave the poolhall, that roomful of bodies,
and shoot Johnny Jones,
                    set him on fire
then watch as the flames rose to smoke, rose as the dead do
and like the dead, drifted in the gauze light of the bruised sky, back to me.
As one by one their stories are told
they fold themselves into the sledged dark and ask the same thing,
track the edges of my body, give me a name.

Will our minds' slips and jumps ever be understood, even to ourselves?
I'm in a deli and suddenly remembering
that more than a decade has passed since I saw my father,
and I don't know what—
a blood-clot in the gray pleats of his brain,
small strokes, DT's or Alzheimer's—stumbled
him through the rooms of my childhood home,
                                drubbed up his hallucinations,
smashed chairs through windows,
raked glasses and plates from the cabinets,
flung food to the floor in his search for boys,
the houseful he was convinced I'd hid.
The way he looked at me, what he said,
                          what I still can't say.

No matter what archangel I've called to my circle of salt
or which words I've cast in the hour of Venus,

the dead have me in their pocket,
                              knotted in a map
whose making I had no part in,
                              and with me is a man turned in his seat

to tell me the government has robbed him,
as if he knows I've felt the sudden suck of a leg in quicksand,
the clang of a beaver trap on my ankle.
He knows the flinty joints that keep me looking for sure ground,
knows that where I grew up
even the smallest rains are floods that redefine the earth,
and land rises in water and turns over on itself.

Is there a place where this transformation doesn't happen?
Where one doesn't wake in the brilliance of reflected light
and the entire acreage of beans vanished under water?

Ask the calf who wandered into Brown swamp never to be seen again,
ask the chokeberry shaking its fruit into the pond of sand.

Or ask this man who must see how I'm marked, shaped
                              by what I lack.

A home-baked apple pie and a woman
                    to rock him in her arms.
He leans closer and whispers this again,
as if he knows while bulbs pushed flesh heads through years of waste,
I have lain in a johnboat
in water churning with mating toads,
thinking of nothing but the pond's depth
and my desire to be picked clean.

He knows I lie down each night in a solitary box of dust
                              and am raised again
only by morning's scour,

knows the trail I follow is not of my making,

                                                that the search defines me.

Signals pass from cell to cell

so I want to join the dead, be one of the hallucinations,

to follow the invisible boys scrambling

through the windows of my father's mind and erased in a brain's blink.

This man who is haunted by women and apple pies—

he knows what it is to want nothing

but a backwards walk through black feathers and moths,

                                                   the salt licked from skin,

knows I long to be taken in the teeth of pondweed,

to leave my body to the river of fog,

                                   the stories to themselves,

to let them fall through nights to an earth too full

and be gathered by those I can't touch, but who touch me,

                                            who touch me.

Sandbar at Moore's Creek

Here where the creek culls sand and silt
and rises against itself

to become something else entire . . .
    here I bring my sorrows
like the delft-blue mussel shells,
fingertip tiny, most beautiful when strewn wide with loss.

If I ask anything of them, if I search for an opening
    as if they were stars in a sand-sky
that fade each night when the real stars
descend to drink the mirror of water,

what does the creek care?

It's day yet:
the light shaking down
through the hackberry branches,

the sky colored raw bone,
    caught on the water's unbroken surface.

Walking the Geese Home

I don't know what patterns itself in their minds,
lifts them in a cry of alarm
then settles them
in a pasture a mile up the road.

Perhaps spring,
                    again without apology,
knowing we will suffer the pat on our heads and the flustered kiss,
as if there had been no abandonment,
                                        would never again be a departure.

With geese, everything is measured by their easy startling;

as if they too are informed by a white rose on the second Sunday of May
or the wink and the word whose lack
I imagine has pitched the black walnut forward through a haze of rain.

The smallest motion pushes them
across the years of inked promises, letters sent from a hospital,
and my mother, a hummed song I almost hear,
spills from mist, comes across the field
                                and takes my arm.

And why not—in spring a uniting seems most likely.
Gnats rise from the clumped grass,
fish begin their slow drift up from the pond's bottom
and bees hover at the hives where hexagonal spirals,
                                        the straining upwards
with their own bodies' waxes, have begun.

Why else this ascension if not practice for a final reknitting?

I've never questioned my grandmother's story;

how three doves clung to the porch screen,
moving their heads side to side as if recalling something forgotten,
then flew off into the moth-white light.

When my grandmother went to the door, there, she insists,

                                was my mother,

unchanged by death,
perhaps brought home by our hopes,
two years after she'd been lowered into the earth's throat.

My grandmother, astonished to silence,
simply watched her walk from pie-safe to fireplace,
studying the shelves of peaches, stewed tomatoes,
corn like fistfuls of baby teeth
and finally out the screen door into the new season

                              where I,

my expectations raised by an arrival,

                    wait.

Is it not true that what we most lack is given back to us by our longing,
pulls us between her knees and runs a pink brush through our hair?

Clouds draw themselves out like a name called from a distance
and oily rainbows ribbon my feet
on a road that one month ago was knee-high in snow.
Six months ago I couldn't get enough of the sycamores
but walked this road in yellow leaf-swirl

                        under limbs peeled to bleached bone.

Now the coming season has flamed the flotilla of branches with blunt buds
as if the dead, when they shift
from the middle world, need the path lit.
They struggle from under windfall and rocks,
swell in their hard shells and twist into light
sharp as memory of spring floods
and seeds rotted in the fields.

The dead refuse to rot,
                            but push their pale faces against soil,
refuse to rot, but climb to the moons in my fingers
and use my nail clippings as wings.

They unfurl through shafts of light,
                            unravel through cloud-wrack.

They come to me from the gleaned fields,
carry the stump that broke the bushhog blade,
the stone that dulled the sickle.

They are the stone dropped in water and circling me to possibilities,
to spring and the way I can't walk even this straight road
for worrying my grandmother's story,
chasing it as I chase the geese,
gathering and starting them again on their uncertain pedaling.

I want to know after my mother walked off the porch, where did she go?
Want to know how to forget the promises,
to forgive the ones who close the screen door for the final time,
who choose a direction to turn and turn,
                            but never toward me

waiting on this road, behind the hesitant, hoarse-voiced geese,
with those who remain trackless and everywhere,
arm in arm with nothing but the freckled wind.

THE SILENCE,
THE BONE-WEARY SOUND

Winter

(in memory: CNHJ)

First light shook with ax-blows to the frozen pond,
and the geese called in guttural distress
as I chopped through to the still, black water.
All day the land gave over to thaw, and snow released the cabin,
softened and eased off the ridged tin roof in foundation-shaking crashes
until night when Orion whistled his dogs
behind clouds mottled like weathered rock,
then the farm sighed under the new storm
and silence returned like an old sorrow.

I wish that silence held some answer or passage
to forgetting. I would go to it
with its hesitant and dangerous tacks,
its seepage into night like shadows slipping into bodies,
where it hangs like smoke,
drifts into itself as smoke will,
rises slow above trees
to the flat of the sky, rises and hangs
and, like sorrow, waits and will not fade.

At Winter's Edge

Hard to imagine the creek without this luxury of destruction,

                                 the dam broken

as if the water squeezed between it and the scrub-choked cliff
thought it a scar to be accounted for,

                     then taken in.

Here where the pleats and creases of the flood-sheared slope

                              are most severe,

a crust of ground rock and silt laces the stones
each time water surges from the failed banks.

In summer, flood-gleaned seed of spurge, creeping cress,
fleshy bulbs of horseradish and sapling bitternut

                         reclaim the slime-slick dam

knotted with weed and yellow bloom.

But not now. The year having rushed to waste—
the hickory pushes toward the current,
blanched vines rot,

           husks whisk in coarse wind

and a spindly-stemmed privet clings
on the dam's cusp in a cove of sand and pebble,
in the rock's contraction and swell.

Each year it's like this: the outward reaches
of sandspit and shaded tucks

                   first to freeze and last to thaw.

Does it matter if ice marks the season's approach or wane?

Grief enough cleaves this wrecked land with beauty.

The privet is doomed.

Fragments in February

Winter barely a month old and already
the Greek cook has ruined a ball point
carving *Fuck This Shit* into the back door's frame,

and John, skunk-drunk, is in the parking lot,
rocked back, shouting,
God. It's me, God. John. His words, like a worn ball,
kicked to the tar-and-gravel roof
he cranes his neck to see over.

                              Does anyone hear?
Ask the broken moon's glint across the blue-black rails,
ask there where they round a curve to invisibility.

There was a time when I believed in train tracks,
believed in the Amtrak sleeper with its billiard-green curtains
swaying with the wheels' gnash along the rails
telling me we all had somewhere to go.

But now Ronald, looking for a fight,
has stripped naked and smashed his face through
all four of the bookstore's windowpanes
and sprints up and down the back alley
where ice catches the moon like scattered glass.

                              ⌒

John is still in the parking lot.
Pizza's late and again the owner has forgotten my name.
Skata re. Skaseh. Malaka American. Skaseh.
Pizza ready you. Shut-up. Deliver.

Being cursed in a language you don't understand,
it's as if nothing were said, not one hurled syllable

limps through the steamy kitchen
or blows its impatient horn spinning out of the parking lot.

Ronald, still naked, has crawled under a car,
lights tunneling toward him,
the police tracking him by the splattered blood.
The cook sings as if,

                 in a different language,
he could make a path.

He's a rich man in the old country,
with a beautiful wife and land,
acres rolling into the mist from the sea.
She won't come to America; he won't go back.

His swollen hands clutch at air to describe this,
then despair and wave it all away.

                       *

I don't know what map I misread,
its roads now slipped into dust,
what cul-de-sacs and one-way streets
could have brought me to this,
my life driven as if through fog into a river.

Soon enough I'll mingle with the catbriars
linking off the tracks, bend into dust
under the graveled roof jutting into the stained light.

But what if I could leave this parking lot,
shake the smell of grease and diesel from my coat,
walk to the road's dead end and scuff downhill
    into the steep woods?
If the woods closed in and the rain-carved gully sloped down,
could I work through the thick vines of fox grape?
If the yellow of the forsythia
force-bloomed by the long, strange warmth

of January has given way to a limp lucidity
and the clavaria is broken and patterned
by running cedar it has struggled up through,
could I continue this stumble over something
                              other than words,

through all the inventions of time
until my final stuttered silence?

When the gully disappears into black mud,
could I break through to the river,
crawl out on the rock ledge and lie over the water
where the banks narrow before a spill of rocks
and the water battered to froth licks up
the stones' mottled faces like flame on wet wood.

Here where the river begins its rush to oblivion,
it is most brutal, the water moiled to opaqueness,
                                        so much not visible,
the untold leaves and windfall swirling in the wash,
                                        then tossed out.

Who knows, here where it's deepest,
what else the river might hold, or what net
I could toss into air as if dragging,
not for something lost, but never had,
pulling against current, as if it were possible,
                              an entirely different world.

But *Fuck This Shit* is carved on that frame for keeps
and even the occasional leaf churned up from dark water,
black and fattened as if caught in the backwash a long time,
topping a brimming crest and tumbling free,
                              doesn't change those words,
never more than partially understood,
but keeping me here,
                    though I know the odds.

The Delivery

I don't remember if a filmed moon floated silver and belly-up in a wash of blue-black or trembled in a cloud-scudded sky that scraped against the roofs. Perhaps it rose slowly as if following me up the stairs and down the breezeway past grated windows and doors bright with eyes. What I'm certain of is the ten the man gave me. That and how he opened the box, pulled out a slice of pizza, green pepper and pepperoni, and put it on the lid as he waited for change. Another man came down the breezeway, said hello, disappeared into the dark apartment then reappeared. Some things can only be said one way. He had a butcher knife and I swear as I watched, he grew; swelled, chest barreled, shoulders flared, his face hardened to mask-like savagery, his eyes beyond doubt, already seeing the world as one who was dead. His right arm hung high over his head. Then everything speeded up, the blurred knife plunged to its hilt and pulled out of the customer's neck, lifted again and one huge drop of blood arced into air, then time returned to normal, and the blood hung, quivered indecisively, then curved like nothing except a huge drop of blood, to splatter on that slice of green pepper, pepperoni pizza.

That's the way it was. The customer stumbled down the corridor. The other man sank back into himself, the knife loose at his side, his face gentle, and seeing me, two feet from him, flecks of blood on my uniform, he seemed genuinely surprised. If there was a moon it might have chosen that moment to sail from rifted clouds. That moment to feather the twisted terraces of ivy in silken light and dissolve the shadows to gray and purple mist. Not that I would have cared, so slabbed with fear I could not move. I thought *witness*. I thought *I'm next*. I don't know what he thought as we stood a minute, two. Then he spun on his heel toward stairs I had not known were there and I to the opposite stairs, the knifed man, my truck, the hospital.

What's there to say after that? I was told the man turned himself in. Had done the stabbing because his sister was strung out on drugs and being pimped out of the back room. But that was days later, hearsay from another driver, three A.M. Who could see the moon? We were mopping the pizza joint's floors.

44

In the 25th Year of My Mother's Death

When the land shifts at day's end
and light sifts slow across field-fetch,
sun smoldering the tombstones cresting
the near hill in a small wind
ripe with weed and rot,

my mother, no longer caring
how day gathers into itself,
does not step from the back porch
to watch the blue heron
reel above the sedge, hover
then plunge into the rising mist.

Soon pines drop from the horizon;
lamplight doesn't seep across the lawn
through air no one breathes
which fills with the scent of apples
and the pitch of apples, snapped stem
and branch, to the root-buckled earth.

Bruised useless, they're not lugged to the horses.
Geldings, sold to buy a casket,
don't stride shank-high through pond grass,
climb dripping from the banks
and shudder like a sleeper
shaking off dream.

In this ebb and sigh of dark easing all around,
no one searches the sky
for Antares burning the Scorpion's heart
or hears the bobcat's cry like a woman's scream,
exactly like a woman beyond any words.

Silences

That summer the burning dump snagged scuffs of smoke against air
that tasted like chicken houses and pig-muck
and, with each spasm of wind, like the rotting
blood-rucked pond south of the abattoir.

Regret must taste like that,
                              sidewinding
and blotch-bodied,

or sound like the scrape of brogans,
and a shovel's chunk and slam
                              in the distance.

It must wait somewhere in the bootheel of North Carolina.
Regret is Peanut McPhee. Four lanes of highway leaving him
with nothing but a leer, he'd twist his leg-stump
onto the check-out counter of my father's store
and laugh about how he used to prowl the back roads
hoping for blacks needing rides,
then he'd jam his crutch onto the gas pedal,
burst onto Highway 74, slue into oncoming traffic,
jolt through ditch-scrub and front yards,
all the time cursing the pleading man in the backseat.

It's a line of men,
                    black men,
sunk-eyed and swollen-faced,
digging in the heavy clay in bloated silence.

And as the two-lane becomes four
in the shackled summer hours of god's sleep
under the guard's gunmetal gaze
                              at the shank-end of the century,
it slinks past, into the haze-shot horizon.

From my father's store I could hear the screams
of the cows surging along the plank.walkway
from the holding pen to the damp room
where Big John waited
for the massive scaffolding of forehead,
the curled eyelashes and those eyes
he'd rock a twelve-pound sledge between.
Then a hooked hoof, pulley and slash, tied intestines,
    the saw's sundering
and the final hosing of the waste
through the rusted grate.

The summer I was twelve a bull heaved backwards,
broke through the chute,
jumped five feet to the ground
and galloped into the store yard.
Big John right behind in the truck
locked up the brakes, wedged his shoulders
in the window and raised a rifle.

How slight the distance
from that mass of black hurtling through air,
muscles bulging and lengthening,
tearing dirt and grass at each thrust,
                            to a buckling plunge,
the knife's twist into the throat,
the hook and winch and drag to slaughter.

This was years before we'd know about
the blood seeping into the water filtering plant.

When I was five, my mother took me to the water plant,
where Mr. Little, pouch-eyed and warty, showed me

the low brick wall on the fifth floor to lean over
and look through twenty feet of water
                              to the final filter,
a sinuous sheet of sand it had come up through.

He said if I fell in I'd keep sinking
                              layer after layer,
and I saw myself tumbling spread-limbed through water
as if falling was all I'd ever known,
born never hitting bottom, always fumbling
through the same explanation,
as if this time, maybe

maybe I'd find that defining moment
I will always answer to.
A moment somewhere back there
with words which slip through asphalt
and regret coiled in the thick twists of ditchweed.
Years on years I've searched
that day I kicked my eight-year-old legs
against the paint-peeling store bench,
while the bored guards
clicked on, clicked off their rifles' safeties.

Maybe if I knew the name of that one machine
squatting above the holes it dug,
stub-bodied, shuddering and grappling with the earth,
spitting vicious breaths of tarred air.

Or maybe that moment is in that line of men,
the sun spangling off the chain links,
their hands twisted to the smalls of their backs,
pushing themselves to a slumped sickle-curve
to stare toward the dirty windows of Jordan's Grocery.

Or as the highway crawls belly-down through dust
under a sun that hunkers even the weeds

and pins the spawn of ash in the west—
maybe it's in the silence, the song they didn't sing,
the bone-weary sound they made when they did not cry out.

DREAM OF THE END

Dream of the End

How soon we've come to our own molded moon
and the knucklebone's length between it and the three suns.
As a horned crescent it forecast storms.
When caught in silk and a bucket of rosewater,
it told maidens how many days before marriage.
But now it's flung to the smeared west.

The other moons practice abandon as few have seen.
They are garibaldi and fantail, rock beauty and skink's skin,
and the last, the seventh moon,
east of the three suns, is a translucence,
an idea on the eye's opposite side,
the color of dream, color of a web's slow unweaving.

Our memory swells the chest of the frigate bird,
then leaps amaranthinian
to yellow sea slugs and an acorn split to pale root.
Only memory runs from the fields to save the gray mules
or hear the stamp of horses, pale and red.

⁀

                                        If I could, I'd wake
and go to the rusted mailboxes dizzy in their coils of wire,
to the night gathering its bones from the black rails,
the crows called to their second lives
and storm drains swallowing the bright and rabid eyes.

What significance the feather hurled into my path from the black-winged sky
or sleep one night to a moth frantic at my window,
the next to snow's slantwise plummet in wind?

There's an alley where old men in stained undershirts
lean from their windows above the stores
near where the Amtrak slows

in the curve before the bridge.
Awake and arms akimbo, I could walk down those rails,
tightrope-step language to language
to the kitchen where the new cook,
a cousin from Greece, begs for sex.

You and him, he says.
If not, then you and another woman.
I can join, he says.
And finally, you and another woman.
I'll just watch, he says.

The alley trash cans reconfigure themselves
and another bag arcs toward the dumpster,
spiraling the screaming birds from the pavement
scabbed with bread crusts and broken beer bottles.

There in the distance, a pale face.
What person, with a shrug, turns away?

                    If I could, I'd wake
from this sleep of names,
Elam, Babylon, Ninevah, America.

                              But I sleep and in sleep I unravel,
scour roadsides for weeds and eat tomorrow's casket spray.
No more discing, no gray mules to save.
I wait with yellow eyes under the bed,
twirl with the deer teeth on their string.

I can say these people have been traced to the river valley,
can say it has been thirty millennia,
but the crippled dog calls from the side yard,
the owl from its rotted tree.

The dead understand this and hang around.
They throw instructions scraped from the night,
count my teeth and ready the boat.

Steady in candlelight I chant what words I can,
for who can say which, if any, belief will save us.

This is an end without reason.
These are not words but a poor translation.

What pyramid's tip will lift us to the sun?
What magic give our language to the dead?

I can say Neptune is in Capricorn, Pluto in Scorpio,
I can say I'm the surefooted sign,
the sensible one.

I can palm my pocket of quartz,
vitreous stone, clear as an eye's center
even as we harden, hinge to our own destruction.

Will the eight limbs save us?
Full lotus and my mind steady,
but will the water return to the gravel bed,
the spider its web?

Rune light and no light. Owl screech in shunt light.
A slide step, circle of salt, and the sink to deep moss.
Another ritual, another tattered secret flapping in wind.

Red-eyed Beelzebub and vain Gabriel
shooting craps by the cemetery gate.

Try buck goat's blood and cat's gall,
candle blown out by a man newly dead.

Hanged man's teeth and widdershins to the bat's dance,
the night's skit raised through a star's shed blood.
Strappado-hoisted, we're hawthorn pierced in weedy gauze.

Of course, none of it works.
No pale face shifts from the dark,
not even a stranger who shrugs and turns away.
Soon we'll all be otherworldwise
and the preacher hang like a horse thief.

Sinaloa to Nayarit,
Culiacán valley and the long rows of tin shacks,
Santiago Ixcuintla and its tobacco,
the Huicholeo Indians asleep under the strung cords of drying leaves.

Who would have thought death's chemicals would smell like vanilla?

Hamivel, Methomyl, Paraquat, Parathion,

Adrian Allesquita Sota, dead,
Luciano Lomeli,
Alberto Leon,
Jose Luis Santos, all dead,

Malathion, Methamidophos, Endosulfan.

Cuidado Veneno
Altamente Toxico

Margarita, the bean of her casket in the dry earth.
My favorite, Margarita, little daisy.

I could not chase her from the fields
when she snuck out under
the bone stare of the bosses
but gave her the last of my canteen
though my own lips cracked
and the fist of dust stopped my throat.

I tucked her inside my shirt
when the planes flew low
to drop the yellow crop dust.

And though I curled my body over hers,
it was she the sickness found.

Old women came, black shawls
pulled close over dark faces.

I could cut out my own heart,
give it to a *hacendado* to have her back,
and he would tear it apart,
scatter it to the four directions of the leached earth.

Old women shell beans to their laps.

They've seen the children curl into hunger
like supper scraps thrown to the dry wind,

and now the children and unknown diseases.
The iguana in the bushes,
a dog scratching in the yard's dust.

The mockingbirds sound like old women crying.

Vulcan and Vertrac. Rockwell's Rocky Flats.
Dioxin, PCB, PVC, organochlorine.
Magic circles useless in the hour of Mars, fourth moon wax-
ing.

The dead long since finished falling
and still we scratch our names in their sweat,
sweep them down with the raffinate and the nine-legged frogs.
We wash in the yellow water, eat the eyeless chicken.

A brew of greed and Atrazine,
a red-bellied spider between buttered bread
and a mother buries her child.

~

        If I could wake
I'd walk into this November night,
into this century still as newsprint and ending,
pass doors blank as statue's eyes,
through the leaves' metallic click,
walk into this darkness,
the long winter, hunch-shouldered as a bat, above us.

At the wharfs no one answers the wind's one question
to the worm-slick wood
or knows what sifts from the night
and startles the sleeping birds to noise.

Only the termites carve our history into the piers,
only rats layer it in nests of straw and debris.

A moon like a glass eye, staring and sightless,
memory that grows false,
and bones. Always bones.

But I sleep and dream of the moon's mule-whiskey drunk,
the anvil shot of the raven falling from night's pockets
and our inconsequentiality
stubbing beside the swollen bodies
dumped into the river with the two-headed fish.
Dream of a cat's dirty fur and a chuffing cough,
twist in the winding sheet of starlight a year or a millennium coming.
How to know if they or we still live?

Tell me a story, the round-headed boy said,
and I did, by god, in this year of our lord,
war oncoming from all sides. Why wouldn't I?

In the night of the soul's dance across luminous skulls,
it's the land that inherits me by the bulked black end.